ME? START A DREAM GROUP?

ME? START A DREAM GROUP?

Non-fiction, Educational

CAROL OSCHMANN

Carol Oschmann

CHAPTER 1

Introduction

Inside, you'll find what prompted me to start a dream group some ten years after I started working on my dreams with no help from anyone. There are things I learned from my dreams. There are many instances when I spread out to dream for others. You'll find a way to start this yourself or in your group. There is a reference to my group I taught in a federal prison and the things I could share with them. Whether or not you start a group, you'll learn much to help yourself along the way, including bringing dreams back and getting answers to life's questions straight from the source.

CHAPTER 2

Why and How

My first dream group came about because the people around me, neighbors, people in my church, and my community all thought that I was crazy for talking about my dreams. I knew I was not. God was improving my life by talking to me in my dreams. I wanted to tell everyone so they could do it also.

People wouldn't listen. They were not interested in dreams. Times have changed, and one shouldn't have that problem today when more people are eager to talk about dreams. There are still unbelievers. I needed someone besides my family to cut me some slack, to say that perhaps I was onto something.

Eager to find someone I could talk to, I put an anonymous ad in the local penny saver asking anyone who had nightly dreams and wanted to talk about them to call me. Only my phone number would identify me.

I got three calls. We agreed to meet at a local cafe. Two of the women brought friends, also believers. Six of us decided to meet weekly, as our dreams were nightly. Later on, men were also drawn to our group.

None of us were experts on the subject. All we had to begin with were our dreams and what we'd learned from them, if anything.

When one of us was stuck on a dream's meaning, we all chipped in and told, based on our own experiences, what the dream might mean if it were ours. We became thankful for the added ideas, as they solved a lot of things we needed help understanding.

Why, today, should I even start a dream group when I can research my dreams online or in one of the many books on the subject? That's just it. There are many ways to interpret your dream. Each book on the subject tells of one person's experience or ideas. In a group, you have the experience of several people to draw on.

Each person may have ideas about the meaning of the objects in the dreamer's dream. Only the dreamer will know the truth when it's mentioned. Only the dreamer is living their life and has had their experiences. Hearing someone else's idea that might bring up that "ah-ha feeling," they'll also say, "Of course, why didn't I think of that?"

The interpretation books do sit quietly by, as does Google, for the time when we are all stuck as to meaning. The books might jog something we'd not thought of. We still do not take them as gospel. Only the dreamer knows for sure what the dream means.

In the beginning, I had access to either a blackboard or a tripod with paper on it. I'd write out enough of the dream being told (in the center of the area) to jog our memories. My Zoom group has taken on the task of writing their own version of the dream. Your people might want to bring a pad and pen to group and do this writing and listening for themselves.

Then I'd circle the important words or phrases, draw a line out to the side and we'd work on them separately. We'd work on each as if it was a separate message from the dream. My suggestion at the time was to write their nightly dreams the same way, in the middle of the page, to leave room to work on possible symbols later.

In a group, you become intimate and get to know each other well. It's a knowing of shared intimacies, of authentic, safe friends who only want good for each other. You each are looking to lead the best life that you can. We all are only human, and we make mistakes. This goes without saying. Once an error is brought to light, we rely on the dream to set the dreamer straight.

When offering an interpretation, I initially tell my group, "Do not tell anyone how to live their life." We always preface our remarks with the phrase, "If it were my dream, it would mean ....."

CHAPTER 3

My First Group

You might not think of yourself as a scholar of dreams. In my first twenty years of dream work, I led dream groups based on what I learned in my dreams. If there is a food in your dream, you either take it out of your diet or add it. The symbol can be healing in more ways than one. It's there in your dream for a reason. After that, I attended an accredited dream school (Haden Institute) and learned much more.

In the beginning we were a group of like-minded people who dreamed a lot and remembered our dreams. We found each other from a simple classified ad I put in the local paper. I also gave invitations to people I knew with these instructions: pass it on if they were uninterested. Possibly, they knew someone who would be interested, someone who had a lot of dreams.

The dreams themselves will bring images. The meanings are known only by each member and are personal to each member, but the thoughts need jogging. You can share your definitions in a group when you hear someone else's dream. The image might now hit home with the dreamer who had never looked at his dream or life in that manner. You can use a dream dictionary or two. I found visitors to the group often brought their own dictionary. You can't rely on them alone. Dreams come for each individual.

For instance, you can ask questions about the dream to clarify what they think about frogs if they are in the dream. Perhaps a person they know also shows up in the dream. Why that person and not another? We might ask for three personality traits of this person as the dreamer sees them. If the person's personality traits seem the same as the dreamers, then look at what that person is doing in the dream. Are you advising yourself? It all has something to do with the message the dreamer needs. It all comes down to the dreamer.

What do you think of frogs, or what do you think of that person? Are you becoming like them? Should you be more like them? Do you share a talent that should be built on to bring you peace or something to the world?

You can meet in each other's homes or in a free room at a church or local library. You might get lucky and have a blackboard. You could also have a list of books to hand out. My favorite fun read is Jeremy Taylor's "Where People Fly and Water Runs Uphill." Jeremy's own dream journal is a rather large book. Each page holds more than one dream. He spends time drawing pictures to illustrate his dream. It's really a work of art! It deals with more than one talent. I hope it's published for all to see. It might be a fun way of journaling for any artists in the group.

I was privileged to take classes with Jeremy and learned several idioms from him. For instance, "dreams use what you know to teach you what you don't know."

When you dream of a familiar situation, like your job or child-hood, look for the "little thing." Eating a live frog sandwich could be all about your diet and nothing about your family in the past or your job now. It might be a comment on something you are taking on your shoulders that you're not ready for. It needs to cook more. We don't eat live frogs!

Another way to use that idiom is explained by the story of a man in my group who was a hospital administrator. Every dream he brought to the group took place in the hospital, even in the hospital's multi-storied garage. We learned to look for the odd thing in the dream and ask him to compare it to something in his life today. He didn't have to tell us, but he came to feel comfortable with us and shared a lot.

The big question is: How do I keep people coming back? The dreams will decide. We hope everyone gets to share, so a small group is best, even five regulars. A person dropping in gives added excitement to the group, as does the occasional dream the regulars are asked by friends to bring to the group. You can always put another ad in the paper if too many people fall by the wayside.

If you are a scholar of dreams or psychology, keep the interpretations simple, following the basic Jungian rules. You might stick to my own experiences that I've shared with you here. You don't want them coming away thinking they don't have the education to dig that deep to find meanings. It's incredible how the surface-level interpretations can hit home.

CHAPTER 4

The Importance of Dreams

Dreams might be more important than you know. Would you want to miss help from your subconscious or even a higher power? Are you living the best life you can, doing what you came into this world to do? A group of like-minded people can keep you focused on your dreams. The dreams need interpreting.

After all, there's an old saying about a dream not interpreted is like a letter unopened – a letter from God or your unconscious. Both only want the best for you.

Some dreams that helped me begin my dream study were right on. I learned to ask my creator questions and get answers. I'd write a question I needed a solution for on a slip of paper, pray over it before bed, tuck it under my pillow, and wait for an answer in my dreams. A lot had to do with my health.

One of my first dreams told me that I was way overweight. My first dream was crossing the Canadian/American border when the border patrol stopped me and wanted to search my car. In the trunk, they found illegal hams. I woke in the middle of the night laughing.

That was no news; I'd tried every weight loss program I could. I wrote my first note to God and asked Him how I was supposed to lose weight. He gave me a direction that I found easy to do and have followed through to this day, but the weight didn't fall. It stayed the same. I asked a second time. I still need the results I wanted. I asked a third time, and I had the correct answer this time. Soon, I lost fifty pounds that I've never gained back.

I hesitate to say what worked for me as our problems are central to each of us. You'll understand when I tell you that the first directive was to give up red meat. It's not for everyone but it kept my weight at a constant level. The one that worked the best was when God showed my marching around the table to country western music (my favorite). God was showing me a way to start to exercise gradually and one that I'd keep up just for the fun. If you can't move, you can enjoy the music while you jiggle to the beat. My abilities grew. Ask God before going to sleep for your own best way to lose weight.

As for the dream symbols, I learned that a car is you. It represents your journey through life. My car in the dream was a Volkswagen punch bug. To me, that was a humble car, not flashy and self-important. That, I'd hoped, was me. I was crossing a border in life. I needed to lose the extra weight to go the right way. Yes, I saw that also. I was going nowhere in life with my choices for all the weight, figuratively and actually. I needed to listen to my higher power.

Through the dreams, God began working on what else was wrong in my life, for instance, my attitude. The dreams helped me with relationship problems and got me on a different path regarding building my self-esteem and choosing a better way of making a living. I feel as if I'm directing the conversations with God.

Soon after these problems were solved, the dreams turned more symbolic. Now, my higher power is catching a mistake I'm making, directing my path, so to speak. If you are close to living the life God meant for you, the dreams turn symbolic. And who's to know what messages we're getting unless we journal and interpret our dreams.

I found this true when I went into a prison to teach the inmates to understand their dreams. They often had totally wrong attitudes, owing to their addictions and the bad things they were led to do. They desperately needed help from a higher power. They got it!

If you are interested in prison stories, read my book "Finding Spirit in Prison Inmates' Dreams." The first version was called "Prison Dreams." You'll find a group of reviews there. If you read "Finding Spirit," please leave a review.

You can take a weird image and ask God for further information. You can ask the next night of dreaming, with a note under your pillow. You can also ask in meditation.

The dreams that have helped some famous people are right on. Maybe the dreamer knew about interpreting. We know the results as we see their lives.

Would you compare yourself to Einstein? Probably not, but he was known to have a cot in his laboratory. For example, when working on a project, like trying to figure out relativity, he'd lie on that cot if he didn't know how to proceed. In his hand were a few tiny metal balls. He held his hand out to the side, and when he fell asleep, the balls would fall to the floor, waking him. He then had the answer to the problem he was stuck on. It's said Edison did the same, as did Tesla and others. If you're an inventor, give it a try.

Whoever thought of putting a hole in the end of a needle to sew? It's written that Elias Howe was stuck with his sewing machine invention. He went to sleep and dreamed of being in a giant tub of water over a fire. Natives danced around the tub, threatening to stick him with long, sharp spears. He woke when he realized that the end of those spears had a hole. He had his answer! And that's how our sewing needles got holes!

Dreams are also suitable for athletes. Jack Nicklaus is said to have improved his golf swing and brought himself out of a fearful slump by practicing his swing in his dreams. Many songwriters credit their dreams with their songs.

It happens with politicians, also. Lyndon Johnson inherited the Vietnam War. He decided to bring our troops home when, one night, in his dreams, he was swimming in the middle of a river. Trying desperately to reach one side, but the current was too strong. He turned around and tried to reach the other shore. That was impossible also. He woke knowing we were not getting anywhere with this war and decided to pull our troops out.

General Patton, of WW11 fame, was a fiery leader. He often woke his secretary in the middle of the night to dictate new troop orders based on the dream he was having.

Perhaps you or someone you know is also destined to develop a new product, become a statesman, or write the next best song or book. Take out that classified ad and announce you're looking for people interested in studying dreams. At your first meeting, share some of these stories. The meeting could be in your home, or a church or library, wherever it's free. You might aim for fifteen people. Some will fall by the wayside, but if you end up with five, that's a significant number to fill two hours with.

If you suggest homework, have them pick up books by or about Carl Jung, the father of inner work. One thought that comes to me now is to include a section of one of the books about Jung as reading homework. If you have the book, copy a couple of pages to make a point the group needs to learn. Ask if the group will use them to expand their interpretation skills.

As for how often to meet, I've always scheduled once a week for two hours. Most of us have dreams every night. If the message is important, it will repeat in a different story until you get it. It can, then, become a nightmare. God has a plan for our lives. The dreams may be less frequent once you get on the right path. I tell my group members they are doing well when they worry about not having dreams for a while. There may be nothing to say to them except someone's coming to visit, or their car needs gas.

Bringing Back The Dreams

In the beginning, we have to work at achieving our dreams. We've ignored God's messages in our dreams for so long that we must work to convince Him that we are serious and will continue. I even resorted to keeping many toys beside my bed resembling dream images, a little car, a truck, a giraffe, etc. It amused my husband, Jim.

I relate trying to remember your dreams with this story. Say you are trying to follow someone down a path to give that person an important message. You call his name, but he ignores you. You pick up a stone and hurl it at his back; he still ignores you. Finally, you pick up a two-by-four and hit him over the head with it. He is you, missing God's messages. The hit over the head is the nightmare you will eventually have in life or in dreams.

My usual advice is to keep a pad and pen beside your bed. Recorders are another aid. On the pad, I put the date and the words "I will remember my dreams." Pray over it and go to sleep. The dreams may not come the first night or not even the fourth. You've ignored

God in your dreams for so long that now you must convince Him that you are sincere. That's my idea anyway.

Be patient and consistent. Dreams will return. Be ready to write them immediately, as they will flit away instantly. No going to the bathroom first. If you share your bedroom, keep a small flashlight to help you see what you are writing.

That's why having a few stories to share, for instance, about Elias Howe and ideas from Carl Jung, known as the father of inner work and dreams, might keep people interested when they struggle to recall their dreams.

Regarding the privacy of your notes, my husband found them mixed up mush. I could find a meaning to that mush. I never had to worry about him looking in my journal and seeing a name, for instance, that would make him wonder why I was dreaming of that person.

I did share my dreams verbally. Jim was very encouraging, especially when my healing from rheumatoid arthritis happened. We knew the changes in my lifestyle brought it about. Catching the dreams and making whatever changes I could played a role in my healing. Again, read "God's Golden Sword..."

Dreaming For Each Other

Another advantage of a dream group is that you have others to ask God a question for you. One of the ladies in our group had a worry about her eyesight. She faced an operation where new lenses might have to be inserted. She asked us all to dream for her. One person came back with a dream of repairing a homemade quilt. The quilt represented her eyesight (the subject of our dreams). One end of the quilt had five colorful, perfect squares. The other had three. Only two needed repairing. She went to her meeting with the doctor with less fear and a feeling she would not have to spend the big bucks.

We've done this many times in my dream groups. One elderly lady had lost her spouse a couple of years before. She could not shake the grief process. She thought of taking her own life.

She asked for the group to dream of an answer for her. I gave her a pad of paper where she put her name and the question, "Why must I go on?" She did this for each person and passed them the questions. That night, I instructed them to hold the paper before sleeping and pray over the question for her. Then they were to tuck it under their pillows, keep one hand on the paper, and go to sleep.

The following week, we returned to the group and told our dreams of that night. We each saw a small part of her life, something we didn't know. One person hit the nail on the head, so to speak. She saw two curly-haired little girls, twins, sitting back to back on an ottoman. They sang and danced to bright, cheerful, Spanish-type songs, like La Cucaracha (the children's song about a cockroach).

We knew the lady was of Spanish descent, but we didn't know that she had twin grand-baby girls. They had curly black hair. She knew now that she had to live for them.

Problem solved.

Personally, I am known for dreaming for others. People in desperation would find me. It's not a game – you're asking God for help. Several times, I could tell a person why they should go on living. I found a better pathway for their lives or perhaps the perfect mate. I enabled them to hear from loved ones who passed.

Two ladies shared a favorite uncle who had passed whom they missed dearly. All my dreams that night were of being in high places, a mountaintop, the top floor of a tall building, a plane. Then the words came, "I had to go." It turned out the man had been a Delta Airlines pilot.

These kinds of dreams, you don't have to interpret. The one you are dreaming for knows the truth when they hear it. Their uncle was happy and could still see them. He was still in high places.

For more of these stories and how I (and you) can do this, read my book on Amazon, "God's Golden Sword as seen in My Dreams For Others."

CHAPTER 7

Privacy and Rules

Be sure to lay down a few rules.

#1: Whatever happens in the group stays in the group. (While privacy is important, sharing the dream work is still essential to influence others to listen to their dreams.) That said, share as much as interests you outside the group, but don't use names in the telling.

#2: We don't tell anyone how to live their lives. To do this, when commenting, offering your ideas on someone else's dream, be sure to preface your words with the statement, "If it were my dream, it might mean ....."

#3: Make sure everyone gets a say. The two hours may go fast. Sometimes, half an hour will be spent on one dream. Whoever gets left out begins the next session so that everyone can tell one of their dreams within two weeks.

#4: Stress the importance of returning to your dreams every two or three months. This way, things you didn't understand at the time will now step forward as predictions of minor things that came later. Perhaps something like someone stopping by for a surprise visit was foretold, and you didn't understand it then.

#5: Make sure everyone understands who Carl Jung was.

CHAPTER 8

Basic Jung and Me

Bring a dream of your own in case no one wants to start. Another thought is to hand out copies of this book. Contact me at oschmann@verizon.net for free downloads in exchange for being on my email list and occasionally hearing about my new books or adventures. Some basic Jungian rules follow. Some may be from my experience, but they all work.

1. Every person, everything in the dream, is the dreamer. When considering the dream, think of those other people or objects as a part of you. Suppose the dreamer says they came home, set a suitcase on the floor, and turned to do something else. This may have happened. But, in this dream world, the suitcase is also the dreamer. If you were the suitcase, what might you be thinking and feeling? What are your greatest fears and your biggest hopes? What's your purpose? These are good questions to ask the one telling the dream. Have them think they are that suitcase.

Also, perhaps you, the dreamer, opened the door in the dream. A new door in your life is opening for you. Be sure to latch onto any opportunity that comes along. Don't hide in the closet, like your so far unknown desires. You never know where it might lead.

2: Along the same line, a house in the dream is also you. If it's a childhood home, it's something about your past that may have to be resolved: a forgiving, an understanding. If you don't know the house, it's still you. The first floor is in the present. If you walk into a kitchen under construction, you are under construction. Nothing to do but be aware of instances in life that might be a lesson from God, like anger, not understanding, etc.

The basement is your unconscious. Really dig into your past. Something is holding you back. Maybe you were told you can't make speeches when God needs you to talk. Perhaps that old anger mentioned before is keeping you from something important.

The upper floors hold more of a spiritual message. Windows are good in that you can see beyond yourself. If there are no windows, it's something within yourself. Or you need to be more confident about something, maybe spiritual.

3: Perhaps in the dream, your neighbor is trimming your bushes. Naturally, a neighbor is doing this, but this is a dream. Of all the men you know, why this person? What does the dreamer think of him? You might compare him with another neighbor or another man you know. Why aren't they trimming your bushes? First, what in your life needs trimming? Then, what is unique about him or his way of cutting the bushes? I always ask for three personality traits. Is he calm, quiet, studious? Or is he one to anger quickly? If it's the second, perhaps there's an urgency to make the change, trimming back something in your life.

4: Jung said we are like icebergs floating in the ocean of life. What we are conscious of and think of ourselves (our ego) is on top of the water. But there's a whole lot more of us under the water!

Our unconscious being holds many mysteries about us, our talents, our purpose in life, the fears we've pushed deep down, and the things we don't want to think of anymore. It also holds the ability to connect with other icebergs under the water. This may be used to explain knowing things before they happen or sensing that someone we care about has a problem.

5: The dream may not always be about you. Someone you know may be in the dream. So, in this case, we call that person. Even if you have to joke about it, tell them they were in your dreams last night. The message may be for them. You remember your dreams, and they don't. The giver of the dream message knows you will pass on the news.

I have a clear example of this. I once dreamed about the town's only grocer. I hardly knew him. There was a celebration in the dream, and his father (whom I had never met) came to me and extolled his son's virtues. "He could be or do anything."

What to do? I didn't know him well enough to strike up a conversation. So, I wrote him a note telling him my dream about his father. As soon as he got my letter (the very next day) he called me. He believed that this was a message from his deceased father. The grocer, I knew, had been toying with the idea of opening a string of little grocery/gas stations and wished he could talk it over with his dad. This message was his father's approval. The last I knew, he had nine such stores. He became an ally in my political dealings surrounding my business, a marina.

CHAPTER 9

The Bible Connection

Last but certainly not least, it deals with the fear of some Christians that dreams are either the work of the devil or not to be taken seriously. Oh, those childhood nightmares! I'm sure that at some point in most people's lives, they've determined not to remember their dreams. We have yet to hear anyone tell us they were necessary. If I had my way, when families gather around the breakfast table, they'd take time to talk about their dreams. That may be a part of my ministry, my books.

In this section, I'd like to address the importance of realizing that the Bible teaches us about dreams. Secondly, we'll talk more in-depth about those nightmares.

The word "dream" is mentioned 134 times in the Catholic Bible. Pastors, the world over, use different verses in the Bible to teach us something. Why not relate the stories of dreams in the Bible? I've taught them to children as exciting stories. As an adult studying my dreams, I found meaning in my own NIV Study Bible for understanding or interpreting my dreams.

Just think of all the hours of our lives that we spend sleeping. While Adam slept, God took a rib and made Eve. What great things is he attempting to create for us while we sleep?

The stories of Jacob teach us that angels bring messages while we sleep. Jacob also teaches us how to handle our nightmares. If a monster chases you, don't run away. Turn and face it. Ask it what it wants of you. You might be surprised at the talent you'd been given at birth to help the world, which you've not used.

One lady told me of a recurring dream of someone chasing her, wanting her purse. As we talked, it became clear that the person chasing her was her son, who'd built a room in his home for her last years. She now knew God was telling her to make the move. I got thank you letters from both her and her son. It was God sending a message. If she'd only understood Jacob's story!

Just as essential for us are the stories of Joseph, Mary and Joseph, Solomon, Jude, Judas Maccabeus, and others. You can read about these Bible dream lessons and where to find them in my book "Biblical Dream Study" or its next version, hopefully due to come out by next Easter (2024). It will have a similar name. It will hold all the same information but be told differently.

Then, last, I want to talk about demons. Perhaps demons are why many people don't encourage their dreams. The devil has done his work well. They exist! This prompts me to tell a personal story and a story from my prison ministry.

Soon after I began to study my dreams, demons came to me (they were ugly with no form we are familiar with). Night after night, I'd go to bed before my husband, who liked to stay up for the late news. The monsters would come, and I'd run out to cuddle next to Jim. When he was with me, they didn't come. One night, I became sick of this game and sat up in bed and shouted, "God! Take these demons away! I've been studying my dreams and making every change I could understand. Take the monsters away."

He did. I was never bothered by them again. That was close to forty years ago. I've never experienced them again. However, the story served me well in my prison ministry.

In prison, the guards sent me a woman who screamed all night, disturbing all that could hear her. She had one wooden eye. She'd been shot as a small child and suffered from demons ever since. I asked her if she believed in God. She replied that she was trying.

She was taking all the religion classes. I told her my story and suggested she try showing God her preference for Him. Be emphatic; shout if she had to!

The following week, she returned with another woman who slept near her. This woman was to be her witness that she had shouted at God and that they'd all slept soundly ever since. For the rest of my teaching there, she attended my class several times and did not report any demons.

At least she and her bunk-mate became believers in God the night it happened. After that episode, maybe some guards and the rest of the inmates, hearing this, also became believers in a loving heavenly father. There was only one other inmate who'd reported demons. This required a different approach, but we beat them. Let God guide you. What I had planned (using the story of Dorothy and the Yellow Brick Road as a dream) was interrupted by something extraordinarily different and funny. As suggested, read my book "Finding Spirit in Prison Inmates Dreams."

If you run into someone who has experienced similar dreams, keep this story in mind. God wants us to be happy, healthy, and wise. Dream groups are an excellent shortcut to understanding the messages from God or loved ones passed. Know what they are trying to tell you.

Happy dreaming!

CHAPTER 10

Books I've Written

Non-fiction
Biblical Dream Study (Interpreting dreams via the Bible)
Finding Spirit in Prison Inmates' Dreams
(Three years teaching dream study in a federal prison)
God's Golden Sword as seen in My Dreams For Others (My story)
He's Not Gone (My dream journal around Jim's passing)
Me? Start a Dream Group?
Fiction
Overboard in Lake Ontario
Soon to be released, 2023 is Devil's Nose
(Overboard book #2)
All are available on Amazon and your Local Bookstore.

My favorite dream interpretation book, The Divinity Code
by Thompson and Beale
(Each image takes you to a book and verse in the Bible where, if
you read the story around it, the meaning of your dream might jump

right out at you. Suitable for solitary searching. If that one doesn't work, try another verse mentioned as a possible interpretation.)

9 7 9 8 8 6 8 9 4 7 3 9 1